BOBBY & AMY

by Emily Jenkins

‖SAMUEL FRENCH‖

samuelfrench.co.uk

FOR AMATEUR PRODUCTION ENQUIRIES

UNITED KINGDOM AND WORLD
EXCLUDING NORTH AMERICA
plays@samuelfrench.co.uk
020 7255 4302/01

Each title is subject to availability from Samuel French,
depending upon country of performance.

Acting Editions
BORN TO PERFORM

Playscripts designed from the ground up to work the way you do in rehearsal, performance and study

---

Larger, clearer text for easier reading

Wider margins for notes

Performance features such as character and props lists, sound and lighting cues, and more

---

+ CHOOSE A SIZE AND STYLE TO SUIT YOU

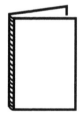

STANDARD EDITION

Our regular paperback book at our regular size

SPIRAL-BOUND EDITION

The same size as the Standard Edition, but with a sturdy, easy-to-fold, easy-to-hold spiral-bound spine

LARGE EDITION

A4 size and spiral bound, with larger text and a blank page for notes opposite every page of text – perfect for technical and directing use

| LEARN MORE | **samuelfrench.co.uk/actingeditions**

Other plays by **EMILY JENKINS**
published and licensed by Samuel French

COOKIES

FIND PERFECT PLAYS TO PERFORM AT
www.samuelfrench.co.uk/perform

ABOUT THE AUTHOR

Emily is a winner of the Fringe First for her play *Rainbow* and had her West End debut with *COOKIES* at Theatre Royal Haymarket. She has written plays for Paines Plough (*Dark Matter*), Traverse Theatre (*The Bed*), Specifiq (*Quarantine*; *Christmas at Newton Park*) and attended the Royal Court Young Writers' and Studio Writers' programmes.

As a director her work includes: *Bobby & Amy* (Upstairs at Pleasance Courtyard), *Serious Money* (Sainsbury Theatre), *Quarantine* (National Maritime Museum), *Vinegar Tom* (Royal Derngate Theatre), *Merry Wives of Windsor* (Royal Derngate studio), *KCS* (Southwark Playhouse), *Rainbow* (Fringe First, Zoo Southside), *Mojo Mickybo* (Old Red Lion) and *Fame* (Northcott Theatre).

Emily is also a text coach and Shakespeare practitioner working at Shakespeare's Globe Theatre. Her productions for Shakespeare's Globe include: *The Tempest* (Dir. Jeremy Herrin), *A Midsummer Night's Dream* (Dir. Dominic Dromgoole) and *King Lear* (Dir. Bill Buckhurst). She also teaches at LAMDA and has worked as text coach for the National Youth Theatre company. Productions as text and voice coach include *Romeo and Juliet* for the Ambassadors Theatre (Dir. Kate Hewitt) and *The Tempest* for Royal & Derngate (Dir. Caroline Steinbeis).

AUTHOR'S NOTE

In February 2001 foot-and-mouth was discovered at an Essex abattoir and it quickly spread across the UK. The highly infectious disease, which mainly affected cattle, pigs, sheep and goats, plunged the agricultural industry into its worst crisis for decades. During the outbreak over six-million cows and sheep were killed in an eventually successful attempt to halt the disease. However, the devastation it left behind was much more long-lasting.

The day the cows started burning many communities were changed forever. I grew up in a little village in Gloucestershire and I still remember the day the fields were taped up, buckets of disinfectant were left at every gate and sty, and my friends and I – who had always freely roamed the rolling fields – being suddenly confined to tarmac and concrete. Pictures of burning animals – pyres of them – were then splashed across the news channels and, for a while, no one would eat British beef.

Foot-and-mouth had a huge impact on farms, families, livelihoods, and the UK economy, and yet it struck me that nothing in the theatre I'd seen – or anything, really – was talking about an event that deeply affected the childhoods of so many of us, or about the continuing erosion of a way of life centuries in the making.

So I decided to write a play about it all. To talk about what happened and to celebrate British agriculture, small rural communities and the huge amount they contribute to the wider world. The characters and the town in *Bobby & Amy* are fictional, but the story comes from the events in many towns and villages across the country.

Bobby & Amy is also a love letter to the nineties. To Take That, Tamagotchis, Dip Dabs, and Pog swaps. To Kickers, hair mascara and curtain haircuts. To necklace chokers, stick-on earrings, Hubba Bubba, and Ring Pops. And to friendship. To those friends you make when you think no one in the world will ever understand you. I hope everyone, somewhere, has a Bobby or an Amy in their life.

So here's to all that. And to growing up in a truly magical place where there were cows dotted across every field and the sun always shone!

...Ok, maybe my spectacles are a little rose-tinted, it's still British weather we're talking about.

Emily Jenkins, 2019

MUSIC USE NOTE

Licensees are solely responsible for obtaining formal written permission from copyright owners to use copyrighted music in the performance of this play and are strongly cautioned to do so. If no such permission is obtained by the licensee, then the licensee must use only original music that the licensee owns and controls. Licensees are solely responsible and liable for all music clearances and shall indemnify the copyright owners of the play(s) and their licensing agent, Samuel French, against any costs, expenses, losses and liabilities arising from the use of music by licensees. Please contact the appropriate music licensing authority in your territory for the rights to any incidental music.

IMPORTANT BILLING AND CREDIT REQUIREMENTS

If you have obtained performance rights to this title, please refer to your licensing agreement for important billing and credit requirements.

BOBBY & AMY

After a limited preview run at the Vault Festival 2019, *Bobby & Amy* premiered at Upstairs at the Pleasance Courtyard on the 31 July 2019.

Produced by Emma Blackman Productions and Emily Jenkins

CAST

AMY	Kimberley Jarvis
BOBBY	Will Howard

CREATIVE

DIRECTOR – Emily Jenkins
PRODUCER – Emma Blackman
SOUND DESIGNER – Dinah Mullen
LIGHTING DESIGNER – Holly Ellis
COSTUME DESIGNER – Kaajel Patel
STAGE MANAGER & OPERATOR – Roshan Conn

CHARACTERS

BOBBY

AMY

Other characters played by **BOBBY** and **AMY**:

AMY	BOBBY
GOAT TIFF	GOAT KELLY
SLAYER SLATER	GOAT STACE
KID 2	TUCK
BOBBY'S MUM	KID 1
BOBBY'S DAD	FISHBAR JIM
AMY'S MUM	MRS M
FARMER ROG	UNCLE RYAN
MR PATEL	MS H
BUILDER	COUNCILLOR
	POLICEMAN

This is a multi-rolling, multi-locational play. The characters and various locations should be created by the physicality of the actors without the need for additional props and costume.

There is no interval.

AMY *(to audience)* out back by the fields is the old folly – bright
stone barbed wire and buttercups – inside a rickety ladder
reaching raw to a platform so high up – splintered stone
and warping wood wind their way through spiders' webs
and water stains – at top the sun shoots and splices through
a single window with one large beam butting and jutting
into the light – black and white cows polka dot the distance
in the blue and the green of fields and skies – i'm thirteen
– this is my safe place – this is where i hide

    BOBBY *and* **AMY** *are thirteen.* **AMY** *is hiding in the folly.*

BOBBY hello – who is that – what are you doing

AMY go away

BOBBY what are you doing

AMY shhh

BOBBY why

AMY i'm hiding

BOBBY i can see you

AMY most people don't look up

BOBBY how did you get up there

AMY are they coming

BOBBY who

AMY the goats

BOBBY goats – there's cows just past the mill

AMY just leave me alone

BOBBY why are you hiding from goats

AMY duh stupid they're not actual

BOBBY i don't understand

AMY girls from school

BOBBY oh – i don't understand

AMY shhh – hide

BOBBY three necklace chokers six blue eyelashes five stick on earrings hubba bubba hubba bubba ring pop and two tamagotchis

AMY kelly topper and the tamagotchi tappers – kels tif and stace

The **GOATS** *give out a bleaty laugh.*

GOAT KELLY so he was like so i was like – uh no

GOAT TIFF girl power kels girl power

GOAT STACE my tami has three hearts happy – that good

GOAT KELLY cause you look exactly like stephen gately – not

GOAT TIFF more like mikey – barf – yeh that's good

GOAT STACE urgh mikey's gross

GOAT KELLY talk to the hand inglis like literally

GOAT TIFF yeh coz the face ain't listening

GOAT STACE he done a poo he done a poo

GOAT KELLY whatever

The **GOATS** *laugh.*

AMY *(they wait)* they gone

BOBBY yes

AMY i'm coming down

BOBBY are you going to jump

AMY uh no – i'd break every bone in my body

BOBBY that's what i thought

AMY i'm coming down the ladder

BOBBY but it's not safe

AMY why's your shirt ripped

BOBBY kenny slater

AMY you know slayer slater

BOBBY my daddy works up farm for his daddy – farmer rog – he helps with the cattle and the combine

AMY i heard slayer once fed a kid through the combine harvester – so he did that

BOBBY yes

AMY where

BOBBY hay bails

AMY slayer slater – arms like shockwaves – face like a crater

BOBBY up the black plastic bails – sixteen bottom nine middle four top – top of the pyramid – can see over the hill for miles – slayer slater

SLAYER SLATER you wanker you weird robot pussy wanker you're a pussy get off my dad's bails

BOBBY seventy nine houses one church steeple

SLAYER SLATER hey tuck wassuup

TUCK wathuuup thlayer

SLAYER SLATER AND TUCK wasssssssssuuuuuuppppp

SLAYER SLATER look what we got here – we got weird robot boy

TUCK alwight wobot – cwathy wobot – what you doing on hith bailth

SLAYER SLATER your daddy know you're here

BOBBY forty-eight stones in broken down wall – eighteen loose straws two tractors sixty two –

SLAYER SLATER your daddy thinks you're a moron – he told me – he told my dad – he told everyone down the pub he told – said your mum's a munter and she must have shagged a spaztic to have you – that's what he says

TUCK haha thagged a thpathtic

SLAYER SLATER you gonna get off them bails them's my bails knob cheese

TUCK (*sung*)

GAGAGAGLADIATORS

contenda weady glathiataw weady

SLAYER SLATER AND TUCK three – two – one

> **SLAYER SLATER** *and* **TUCK** *grab* **BOBBY** *and start hitting him.*

BOBBY ow

SLAYER SLATER wanker little baby wanker with little baby penis wanker wanker penis pussy little girl vagina pussy – take that – and that

TUCK and that – ha puthy – puthy penith wanker – wickle bwoken wobot wa wa wa

BOBBY ow – leave me alone get off get off get off

> **SLAYER SLATER** *grabs* **BOBBY** *and shakes him.* **BOBBY** *panics, reaches towards the ground and throws some poo in* **SLAYER SLATER**'*s eyes.*

SLAYER SLATER argh – argh you little – my eye my eye there's shit in my eye – i'm going to get you get him tuck

TUCK i'm wunning and wunning – wait you wickle wobot

BOBBY running running feet slap in cow pat skid and swerve but stay straight – three stripe adidas and flashing trainers catching up then fading fading – across the mud and down the hill then falling – down the slip slide down on to the bump bump scratch bruise tumble tumble thump breathe breath – head pain – hip pain – shirt shirt's ripped – horizontal to vertical and lopsided limp – and then this scrunch of red hair ducking past the mill wheel and over the bridge and into the folly – and that's when i met amy – two nine twelve fifteen

AMY what are you doing now

BOBBY counting

AMY counting what

BOBBY buttercups

AMY why

BOBBY it makes me feel better – numbers are safe

AMY that's stupid – you're weird – i'm going

BOBBY can i come

AMY why

BOBBY i don't know

AMY no you can't i don't know you

BOBBY i'm bobby i'm thirteen years nine months two days seven hours and thirty-three minutes

AMY you don't go to the big school

BOBBY no – i'd like to

AMY i'm going on an adventure after school tomorrow – i suppose you can come too if you have to

BOBBY ok

AMY sleepy cotswold town – market square – river – fish shop – old church famous windows – co-op – farm shop – fields and cows

BOBBY the local secondary school – up the lane – iron gates shield of blue and gold – shrill ring then nine hundred navy jumpers black shoes eight big buses windows banging – boys voices high then low then low then squeak

KID 2 get out of the way dumbarse

KID 1 fuck off weirdo

KID 2 dickhead

BOBBY cower against cotswold concrete

KID 2 you see the rack on clare today – 'parently she's wearing proper bras now – her mum took her to swindon weekend – marks and spencer – the goats saw her

KID 1 mate mate i would have that – i would have that twice – wanna swap pogs

KID 2 yeh and how many girls have you actually had

KID 1 plenty – you know me and stacey did

KID 2 not what she said

KID 1 what

KID 2 *(mimicking)* – where do i put it where do i put it

KID 1 shut up shut up she's lying

KID 2 what i heard

KID 1 shut your mouth or i'll shut it for you

KID 2 sure you don't want to wait till your balls have dropped

KID 1 fuck you – *(to* **BOBBY***)* what you looking at

BOBBY duck squeeze through carpark cars step in dog poo but stay statue – crawl through gravel socks and shoes

AMY hey

BOBBY hey

AMY what you doing down there

BOBBY crouching

AMY you're a freak – get up before someone sees

BOBBY three pairs of black leather kickers – laces tucked in

AMY the three goats

   The **GOATS** *laugh.*

GOAT KELLY ooh look what we have here – aimless amy

GOAT TIFF aw hello aimless amy

GOAT STACE aimless amy

AMY hello

GOAT KELLY who's this aimless amy – is this your boyfriend

GOAT TIFF is that your boyfriend

GOAT STACE he's cute – not

AMY no

BOBBY thigh high socks

AMY knot in shirt

BOBBY jewels in belly button

AMY AND BOBBY glitter

GOAT KELLY what's your name amy's boyfriend

GOAT TIFF yeh what's your name

GOAT STACE what's your name

BOBBY onetwothreefourfivesixseveneight

AMY stop it bobby

GOAT KELLY bobby – bobby – he's ugly – what you looking at
   you taking the piss

GOAT TIFF he's in love

GOAT STACE yeh he's in love

AMY no he's not

GOAT KELLY amy and bobby up a tree

GOAT TIFF k-i-s-s

GOAT STACE i-n-g

They laugh.

AMY no – we're not boyfriend and girlfriend – i don't even
know him

BOBBY you do know me

AMY shut up i don't

GOAT KELLY you know your girlfriend's a weirdo – she's always
hiding in break – under the stairs – in the stationery
cupboard – she's like the school troll hiding away in dark
corners

GOAT TIFF haha troll

GOAT STACE troll

BOBBY i like the dark

AMY stop talking

GOAT KELLY hark at him – you like the dark do you – well
looking at you both it's where you belong – two ugly trolls –
loser double loser *(hands make two L shapes)*

GOAT TIFF as if *(hands make an A)*

GOAT KELLY whatever *(hands make a W)*

GOAT TIFF your mum works in mcdonald's *(M)* and your dad
works in burger king *(W on top of head like a crown)*

GOAT KELLY loser – get the picture *(L into picture frame)*

GOAT TIFF living in loserville *(L into roof)*

GOAT KELLY population – one *(P followed by 1)*

GOATS KELLY AND TIFF you *(point)*

GOAT STACE you *(point)*

GOAT TIFF hold up kels it's slayer – slayer's coming over

GOAT KELLY oh my life – how's my gloss

GOAT TIFF yeh fit

GOAT STACE totally fit

GOAT KELLY alright kenny – like yer curtains.

SLAYER SLATER alright kel

GOAT TIFF alright kenny

GOAT STACE alright kenny

SLAYER SLATER stace tiff – *(to* **KELLY***)* – kels i hear you might go out with inglis

GOAT KELLY might do might not haven't decided yet

SLAYER SLATER he said you let im break one of ya shag bracelets so he fingered you down tennis court

GOAT KELLY so – dun't mean we're married – i'm keeping my options open

GOAT TIFF options open

GOAT STACE and her legs

GOAT KELLY no one likes you stacey – where's your thidekick

SLAYER SLATER tuck – detention – he bunsened emma evans' hello kitty case in third

GOAT KELLY cool

GOAT TIFF cool

GOAT STACE wicked

SLAYER SLATER *(to* **BOBBY***)* what the fuck you doing here robot

BOBBY nothing

GOAT KELLY he's grinning at me like a pervert

SLAYER SLATER fuck off before that smile smacks porcelain and plumbing prick

GOAT KELLY yeh go on kenny bog flush the spaz

BOBBY i'm not a spaz

AMY bobby

GOAT KELLY *(to the theme tune of Pinky and the Brain)* the spaztic – the spaztic – *(***SLAYER SLATER** *joins in)* – and the troll troll troll troll – troll troll troll troll.

AMY leg it – past the bins – through the staff carpark – down the back road – past the church –

BOBBY where are we going

AMY the folly

BOBBY into the dark and spiders' webs – up up up the ladder – settle on slats – so high up – little window – long way down

In the folly.

AMY i hate them i hate them i hate them i hate them i hate them – my lungs feel tight

BOBBY maybe you're asthmatic – it's dusty

AMY i am asthmatic idiot – this is your fault – why couldn't you shut up

BOBBY do you have an inhaler

AMY i want to rip your head off

BOBBY you don't have the upper body strength

AMY i'm crying you're meant to make me feel better

BOBBY how

AMY say something nice

BOBBY i like your uniform – i wish i had one

AMY go away

BOBBY want to meet my mummy – she'll make us our tea

AMY why are you following me i don't even know you – leave me alone

BOBBY oh ok – *(he goes to climb down)* – i really do like your uniform

AMY wait – what kind of tea

BOBBY mummy we're home – mummy – mummy

BOBBY'S MUM *(in another room)* – don't come in here bobby

BOBBY mummy this is amy – can amy stay for tea – mummy come out and meet amy – *(goes to open the door)*

BOBBY'S MUM don't come in here bobby

BOBBY why

BOBBY'S MUM just don't come in

BOBBY why

BOBBY'S MUM i've had a little fall and i don't want –

BOBBY where's daddy mummy

BOBBY'S MUM i don't know darlin' – he just went out

BOBBY i want him to meet amy

AMY hello bobby's mummy

BOBBY mummy

BOBBY'S MUM bobby – i'm a little – i can't make you tea right now

BOBBY can we make our own tea

BOBBY'S MUM yes darlin' make your own tea

BOBBY can we go get fish and chips

BOBBY'S MUM yes go get fish and chips – money's in my purse

BOBBY thanks mummy – love you mummy

BOBBY'S MUM love you too darlin'

BOBBY fish and chips fish and chips

AMY fishbar – corner of the market square – peeling paint – waxy fat – fatty wax

BOBBY daddy hello daddy – are you getting fish and chips too

BOBBY'S DAD what's it look like

BOBBY we're getting fish and chips too

BOBBY'S DAD i can see that – with whose money

BOBBY mummy said we could

BOBBY'S DAD my money that's who – i don't sweat all day labouring on farm for you to 'ave fish and chip suppers

BOBBY daddy this is amy

AMY hello

BOBBY daddy i don't think mummy's very well – she was hiding and she wouldn't let me in

BOBBY'S DAD see you jim

FISHBAR JIM see ya dave – you seeing farmer rog – tell 'im i've held back a steak and kidney

AMY bye bobby's daddy – fishbar jim – skin like grease and breadcrumbs – big fat chippy fingers

FISHBAR JIM alright you alright – what ya having – you have money ya better have money

AMY two fish and chips two tomato spicy space raiders please

FISHBAR JIM alright you're alright – coming right up – sit down there

AMY football on the telly

BOBBY football on the telly

FISHBAR JIM football's on the telly – there y'are then – that's good nosh that alright – i'll keep the change

AMY thank you fishbar jim

BOBBY thank you fishbar jim

FISHBAR JIM bang on – see y'around kids

AMY corner of curb – red sky at night shepherds' delight – we eat our fish and chips

They eat in silence.

why don't you go to school

BOBBY mum says i'm too clever and people won't like me

AMY so you don't learn anything

BOBBY i go to mrs m's house and she teaches me

AMY mrs m – my mum makes out she's mental

MRS M they can't poison me ho no – double wrapped these are – and this old nose can smell arsenic a mile away – rat poison too – opal fruit

AMY green plastic seats and big patterned blankets –ivy crawling through cove and crack – she stands outside all day in sleet and shine

MRS M vultures circling vultures circling – caw caw – pecking and clawing at my sun-dried flesh and bone – give it up mrs m – time to politely go and die mrs m – well i'm not bloody going to – caw caw – opal fruit

BOBBY thank you mrs m – should we do some studying now mrs m

AMY mrs m's crazy – i like her – the sky looks like blood – why do people die

BOBBY because our cells age and stop being able to repair themselves so quickly – or they have an accident which is different but the same – and it's not blood – it's light refracting on particles

AMY no i mean – i'm going home – mum i'm home

UNCLE RYAN hello hello hello

AMY hello mr casey where's mum

UNCLE RYAN why don't you come up and sit on my lap a moment little amy

AMY where's mum

UNCLE RYAN she's popped down village 'all – asked me to mind the fort – pop up 'ere for a mo alright – there we are – aren't i a lucky fella to have such a pretty young lady on me lap – you're a big girl aren't ya – 'ow old ya now

AMY thirteen

UNCLE RYAN thirteen – pretty little amy – listen i've been having a word with yer ol' mum and she's been telling how you been sad these last few weeks since your ol' dad died

AMY he wasn't old

UNCLE RYAN truth of it is she's been sad too – and i can't have two lovely ladies like yerselves being sad now can i – wouldn't be gentlemanlike – so what we've decided to do yer mum and me is i'm going to move in to that there spare room and look after ya both for a bit – just till ya get on yer feet alright

AMY yes mr casey

UNCLE RYAN it's uncle ryan now on alright – we're going to be good friends pretty amy

AMY yes uncle ryan

BOBBY but if he's not your uncle you shouldn't call him uncle – it doesn't make sense

AMY mum told me i have to – mum do i have to

AMY'S MUM i'm at the end of my tether what with your father and you – and you're not cheap – how i'm meant on a single income – selfish that man was off and dying that's what he was – didn't even try ta fight it and me being nursemaid to him week after week – ryan wants to help us – he's a good man and a good friend to us so you do what he says and call him what he likes

BOBBY but he's not your uncle

AMY next day – up top field watching new born calves – why are you following me – why won't you leave me alone

BOBBY you left fourteen and three quarter chips – why did you go and leave fourteen and three quarter chips

AMY i don't like you – you're weird – maybe slayer slater's right – maybe you are a spaztic

BOBBY i'm not a spaztic

AMY yes you are

BOBBY i'm not

AMY are are are – what's that noise

BOBBY rumble and squelch

AMY farmer rog up in his tractor

BOBBY dark black wellies dark green coat dark grey cap bright yellow smile – hullo farmer rog

AMY hello farmer rog

BOBBY this is amy

FARMER ROG pleasure to meet you young miss – how's yer dad mr bobby

BOBBY he had fish and chips last night

FARMER ROG did he now – i had a nice old pie meself

BOBBY we were just looking at the calves farmer rog

FARMER ROG ya like calves do ye

BOBBY yes

FARMER ROG ah well hilda's calving just now – want to watch

AMY can we – really

BOBBY is slayer i mean kenny going to be there

FARMER ROG kenny – yer alright – me son's out with tuck saw 'em smuggle out some cans – won't be back 'til evenin'

swaying and smellin a stink – come on then climb up here by the tyres – i'll give ya a lift

They climb up.

off we go – hold on tight

BOBBY we're riding in a tractor

AMY we're riding in a tractor

BOBBY get to the farm – into the barn

FARMER ROG there's my beauty

BOBBY hilda

AMY she's enormous

FARMER ROG hilda's one of my oldest heifers – this'll be her ninth young'un – oh there she goes – won't be long now – there there my love there there – let's have a feel for ya

> **FARMER ROG** *lifts up the cow's tail and puts his hand inside.*

oh dear oh dear

BOBBY what's the matter

FARMER ROG little beggar's turned inside her – it's going to come out the wrong way – if we can get it out at all – i knew she was too old for another

BOBBY four cows six troughs nine spiders

AMY will she be alright

FARMER ROG i don't know lass i don't know – we're going to have to help her

BOBBY the noise i hate the noise

AMY what are you doing – stop being a baby – she's scared – she needs someone to look after her – what do you do when someone's sad

BOBBY make them feel better – say something nice – but hilda doesn't have a uniform

AMY give me your hand – *(She takes his hand and strokes Hilda with it)* – see you're making her feel better

BOBBY six black patches on hilda's coat

AMY isn't she beautiful

BOBBY yes

FARMER ROG now stand back young'uns – i'm going to have to pull it out

He puts his hand inside the cow.

i got the feet – come on hilda you can do this – hold on i'm going to have to pull and pull hard – one two three

He pulls. The calf comes out. **FARMER ROG** *kneels down beside it.*

BOBBY why's it not moving

AMY what's wrong with it

BOBBY why's it not moving

FARMER ROG stand back

FARMER ROG *starts to hit the calf.*

BOBBY what are you doing – you'll hurt it – why's he hitting it like that – stop him

FARMER ROG *starts hitting the calf and shaking it.*

AMY i think it's dead

BOBBY no it's not dead it's not

AMY oh please don't let it be dead oh please oh please

BOBBY no no

AMY i can't look

BOBBY farmer rog what are you doing

FARMER ROG wait

BOBBY why have you stopped

FARMER ROG wait

BOBBY it's moving – amy it's moving

AMY what – and the calf gave out this little cough and started wiggling about – he's alive

BOBBY he's alive

FARMER ROG she's alive – and a nice fat healthy thing she's going to be and all

BOBBY really

FARMER ROG well done old hild

BOBBY well done old hild

AMY well done old hilda

FARMER ROG so what you two going to call her

BOBBY really

FARMER ROG aye – you helped hilda out of a tricky situation – she wants you to name her

AMY i don't know – what do you think bobby

BOBBY abigail

AMY abigail – why abigail

BOBBY because i like it

FARMER ROG all right then abigail it is

BOBBY abigail

FARMER ROG i've got to go check on the herd – will you take care of abigail for a mo – you can feed her with this

BOBBY a baby's bottle

FARMER ROG all creatures need mother's milk – there ya're – sit her up on you and she'll suck away on that – back in a jiff

They sit on the ground stroking and feeding the calf.

AMY abigail

BOBBY abigail

AMY she's the most beautiful thing i've ever saw

BOBBY eight spots and a freckle on her nose – i like her wobbly legs

AMY i like everything – she's going to be so happy – she's going to be surrounded by lots of cow friends all the time and she'll just chew grass and play in the fields and she'll never be lonely

BOBBY are you lonely

AMY sometimes i'm lonely – sometimes more than sometimes – but sometimes

BOBBY you're not really lonely

AMY i am

BOBBY lonely people have no friends and you've got me and i will be your friend forever if you want

AMY why

BOBBY if you want

AMY ok

BOBBY ok

AMY i'm sorry i called you a spaztic

BOBBY i'm not a spaztic

AMY i know

BOBBY every day – up the field watching abigail

AMY growing and growing the most beautiful cow you ever saw

BOBBY each day after amy finishes school we help farmer rog in the farm and he teaches us lots about the farm and cows and everything

FARMER ROG my family been farming this land for generations – my daddy and his daddy before him passed down man to son

BOBBY farmer rog did you know that crops take up over four and a half million hectares of land which is the same as –

AMY bobby no one cares

BOBBY i do it's interesting

AMY no it's not

BOBBY it is – i read it

AMY wait – man to son – farmer rog does that mean slayer slater is going to be a farmer and have this farm

BOBBY and abigail – will slayer have abigail

FARMER ROG aye that's right – now get away with ya – time for tea

BOBBY but i don't want him to have abigail

AMY neither do i – off home for tea – ms huntington-smythe – up on her horse clip clopping heels dropping not stopping

MS H tally ho you young scallywags – open that gate for me there's a good girl

AMY yes ms huntington-smythe – ms huntington-smythe can i learn to ride

MS H ah you want to feel the wind whistling in your ears do you – the mud splattering and spitting your nostrils do you – twenty pounds will give you an hour on any strong steed – cheap at the price i tell you – nothing like a stallion between your legs eh young lady

AMY twenty pounds –

MS H shut that gate behind us – toodle pip

AMY but i don't have twenty pounds

BOBBY i don't like horses – they poo when you're sittin' on them

AMY autumn nearly winter – abigail's coat is thick to stop the cold

BOBBY at my house – watching tv – pass me a smartie

AMY *(She throws a Smartie at him)* here

BOBBY hey

AMY want another – *(She throws another)* – and another –

BOBBY ouch – take that

> **BOBBY** *and* **AMY** *throw and duck Smarties, giggling.*

BOBBY'S DAD what the fuck is this

BOBBY hello daddy

BOBBY'S DAD pick them up now

BOBBY want a smartie daddy

BOBBY'S DAD give

BOBBY we're watching *Get Your Own Back* want to watch with us

BOBBY'S DAD *Get Your Own Back* – sounds like something ya mum would like *(burps)* – she in

BOBBY she's in the kitchen – you been working farm today daddy – did you see abigail

BOBBY'S DAD been putting the lights up in the market – november's too early you ask me

BOBBY and the tree

BOBBY'S DAD aye – it was a bugger but the fucker's up

BOBBY let's go look

AMY not now – i start my new job tomorrow

BOBBY co-op next to fishbar

AMY stack stack

BOBBY shop bell and tinsel – ding ding rustle rustle

The **GOATS** *laugh.*

GOAT KELLY no way – the troll's got a job in co-op

The **GOATS** *laugh again.*

AMY hello kelly – tiffany – stacey

GOAT KELLY aw amy you look so pretty in that tabard – psyche – i'd have thought you'd get a job with fishbar jim – could batter a haddock with the oil on your face

GOAT TIFF haddock

GOAT STACE haddock

GOAT KELLY two packets of marlboro lights – double dip double dip drumstick dip dab and three bacardi breezers

AMY i have to see ID

GOAT KELLY what did she say to me

GOAT TIFF as if

GOAT STACE what did she say – *(playing with Tamagotchi)*

AMY i can't give you cigarettes or alcohol unless you have ID

GOAT KELLY you know me

AMY i know you're under age

GOAT KELLY is she serious

GOAT TIFF are you serious

GOAT STACE are you serious

GOAT KELLY give it to me now troll

GOAT TIFF give it to her

GOAT STACE give it to her

GOAT KELLY or i'll make your face even uglier

GOAT TIFF not possible

GOAT STACE not possible – oh naughty tami

GOAT KELLY put that thing away stace

GOAT TIFF tragic

GOAT KELLY give me them breezers

AMY i can't it's against the law

GOAT KELLY now troll– (**AMY** *hands them to her*) – that's a good troll – come on – slater's said he's built a snowman just for me – bye troll

GOAT TIFF bye troll

GOAT STACE bye troll

BOBBY'S MUM bobby darlin i need to talk to you

BOBBY mummy your eye is bruised

BOBBY'S MUM the angel fell off the tree – bobby have you thought about what you'd like to do

BOBBY i'm going to see abigail and amy later

BOBBY'S MUM no – when you're older – when you've done your exams – have you thought about university

BOBBY university

BOBBY'S MUM you're a very clever boy darlin' – cleverer than most

BOBBY i can remember a lot of things – can amy come with me

BOBBY'S MUM i don't think she can darlin' no

BOBBY but she's my friend

BOBBY'S MUM you can make lots more friends at university – and it's some way off

BOBBY i won't go if amy can't come with me

BOBBY'S MUM dave speak to bobby

BOBBY'S DAD university – and who's paying for that – fuck that bobby – get a job and make yourself useful for once in yer life

BOBBY ok dad i'll make myself useful for once in my life

BOBBY'S DAD i'm off down pub

BOBBY'S MUM i'll leave some bolognaise on the hob

BOBBY'S DAD leave what you like

BOBBY into the pharmacy – hullo mr patel can i have a job mr patel

MR PATEL hello bobby – a job – how old are you

BOBBY fourteen years three months two weeks three days and amy says i shouldn't tell the hours and minutes

MR PATEL do you have pharmaceutical degree

BOBBY no

MR PATEL ah that might be a problem

BOBBY but i want to help people

MR PATEL that's very kind but it is not enough

BOBBY i can remember things

MR PATEL what can you remember

BOBBY seretide asthma evohaler contains fluticasone and salmeterol and norflurane – side effects include headaches thrush aching swollen joints –

MR PATEL goodness – ok ok - do not tell anyone you are not qualified

BOBBY thank you mr patel – pots and pills and words and words and powder and liquid and solid and –

MR PATEL very good work today bobby very good very good – tomorrow antihistamines

BOBBY thank you mr patel bye mr patel

MR PATEL work work never shirk bobby

BOBBY work work never shirk mr patel – into co-op – shop bell – ding ding – hi amy

AMY hi bobby

BOBBY shall we go see abigail today

AMY the snow's thick

BOBBY i got my wellies

AMY up past the christmas tree

BOBBY the spineless old christmas tree

AMY hello fishbar jim

FISHBAR JIM alright alright football's on telly

AMY we're going to see abigail fishbar jim

FISHBAR JIM alright alright bang on – wait – yer going to farm – haven't you heard –

AMY crunch on – past the park – down the lane – over the bridge and into the –

BOBBY what's that

AMY big white sign – big red words – tape across the gate

BOBBY footpath closed – entry prohibited

AMY big white tub with greeny yellow liquid on melted snow on ground on grass

BOBBY why can't we go in

AMY i don't know – let's try the other way – trudge trudge – tape and signs tape and signs – back gate

BOBBY entry prohibited – white and red – field taped up like a christmas present

AMY what's that smell

BOBBY a thick cloud sits on the ground

AMY something's burning burning black up by the farm – quick – through here

BOBBY but it says –

AMY farmer rog might be in trouble

BOBBY through the gap

AMY duck and weave and run up fields kick through hedgerows and up and up and up

BOBBY burning and smoke and yellow and orange

AMY up and up – slip slide and crunch – black on white like old films

BOBBY sweet sick dirty smell

AMY coughing and spluttering – i can't see –

BOBBY black outline of farmer rog at the top of the hill – farmer rog farmer rog are you hurt

FARMER ROG who' s that – you shouldn't be here get away with ya

BOBBY are you ok farmer rog

FARMER ROG didn't you see the signs – you can't be in here

BOBBY are you hurt

FARMER ROG if anyone found out – contaminated you are now the both of ya

BOBBY we were worried about you – why is there a fire

FARMER ROG i've had to burn them bobby

BOBBY burn what farmer rog

AMY what's burning farmer rog

BOBBY it smells really bad

FARMER ROG aye it smells rotten – it's rotting my very bones

BOBBY what is it –

AMY oh bobby – look – flames and smoke and hoof and skull fat crackling and skin shrivelling red blood shining gold –

BOBBY the cows – they're in the fire –

AMY oh no no – abigail

BOBBY abigail – abigail – amy farmer rog has gone mad – abigail

AMY bobby no

BOBBY abigail – what have you done

FARMER ROG it weren't my fault bobby – it weren't my fault – government came last night – paper suits and paper shoes and a shot gun in them paper gloves – went right round the field they did – nine inch nail straight between the eyes – bang and thud bang and thud across the fields for miles – abigail hilda spots the lot of them – then they left – left that herd strewn across the land not even cold and still spasming

BOBBY abigail

FARMER ROG aye – aye – my great great great great great granddaddy started that herd – man to son – gone in half an hour

BOBBY where's slater

FARMER ROG he's away inside with his mother – i couldn't have them see this – i feel ashamed bobby – so bleedin' ashamed

AMY farmer rog clears his throat – we look away – out across the field – red riddled silver snail trail streaks from polka dot puddles each snaking up and into the flames – he had dragged every last one up the field and into the fire – empty petrol cans sit shimmering round our feet – the fire just laughs and laughs – i see a face in the flames wink at me – the eyeball flops and drops – darkness falls and stars come to squint and blink as the clouds cover the moon but we don't see it – all through the night we stand there as the flames eat our eyes – morning comes – the fire dies – and all that's left is dust and bone we help farmer rog sweep skulls and ashes into black plastic bags and pile them on to the trailer – something inside us has sunk and shrunk – we walk down the hill in silence – we go to our folly – oh bobby – the folly's taped up too

BOBBY argh

AMY cold crack bang against brick and bobby shakes earthquake as his fist pitches against solid stone

BOBBY i hate it i hate it

AMY bobby

BOBBY go away amy go away go away go away go away

AMY his shadow sprints over the hill – i have nowhere to go except home

AMY'S MUM oh ryan oh ryan

UNCLE RYAN oh sandra sandra

AMY'S MUM oh ryan oh ryan

UNCLE RYAN oh sandra sandra – amy

AMY'S MUM amy – what the fuck

UNCLE RYAN shit shit –

AMY'S MUM get out get out get out

UNCLE RYAN fuck fuck

AMY'S MUM don't you judge me – yer dad's been dead for months

UNCLE RYAN come back pretty amy

AMY'S MUM fuck the little bitch – come back 'ere emerald eyes

AMY running and running – tears drip snot licks – um – hello bobby's mummy – is bobby in

BOBBY'S MUM hello dear – you saw farmer rog i understand

AMY yes – is bobby in please – i need to see him

BOBBY'S MUM bobby amy's here – oh – he's um not feeling very well – maybe tomorrow

AMY oh – sun rise splits shadows – i spend the day pacing pavement – cuts and corners gurgle gossip about farm and flames – abigail's eyes hilda's hooves bubble and burn in the back of my brain – sneak back late but mum is waiting –

AMY'S MUM you have to understand amy there are some things between a man and a woman – i have needs – and your father he never – your father wasn't a man – he wasn't even an excuse for a man – at the end he was nothin' but a bag of bones and a flaccid – but ryan ryan makes me feel like a woman – he's dead amy – your father's dead – dead so long he's ranked and rotted – it's time you let him go – let me go – don't you want me to be happy – oh you're still up

UNCLE RYAN i was waiting for this little one – we was worried pretty amy – know it must've been a bit of shock yer ma and me

AMY'S MUM yes well we've had a talk

UNCLE RYAN ah well that's good then – now it's about time we were all in bed – can't have my two gorgeous girls missin' their beauty sleep – how about i tuck in little amy for yer and i'll be right in

AMY'S MUM oh ryan we're so lucky to have you

UNCLE RYAN no i'm the lucky one

AMY a few days later

BOBBY hi

AMY hi – how's your hand

BOBBY my mum wrapped it up

AMY i came over

BOBBY my hand was hurting

AMY are you mad at me

BOBBY no

AMY ok

BOBBY it's ok if you don't want to be friends any more

AMY what do you mean

BOBBY because i shouted at you and then didn't want to see you when you came to my house

AMY oh

BOBBY friends shouldn't shout at each other and i shouted at you so i know we can't be friends any more

AMY oh

BOBBY but you're my best friend amy

AMY you're only my friend because you don't have anyone else

BOBBY that's not true – even if i had a million friends you'd still be the best

AMY no i wouldn't

BOBBY you would – always

AMY i don't like it when you shout at me

BOBBY i won't ever again i promise

AMY cross your heart

BOBBY cross my heart how

AMY just – promise

BOBBY promise

AMY ok

BOBBY ok – town hall meeting – talk of the town

AMY me and bobby with bobby's mum behind rickety plastic table and white china – everyone is there

BOBBY farmer rog

AMY tired and sad

BOBBY fishbar jim and ms huntington-smythe

AMY bobby's daddy – my mummy uncle ryan mr patel even mrs m –

MRS M snivelling bastards – shrivelling and snivelling – it's a conspiracy i tell you – kill the cows – what for eh – power over the proletariat that's what – bourgeoisie bleedin' bastards bleedin' our bones – caw caw – opal fruit

AMY the goats bleat in a corner and slayer slater sits silent by his dad

BOBBY tuck keeps trying to catch his eye – slayer makes him miss

AMY we stay back behind the clink of crockery bite of biscuits – crumbs spit from lips and metal spoons stain brown – wipe and pour and clean and pour –

BOBBY hello mummy

BOBBY'S MUM bobby darlin'

BOBBY what happened to your cheek mummy

BOBBY'S MUM nothing darlin' – come help me fetch more saucers

BOBBY yes mummy

AMY bobby wait don't leave –

UNCLE RYAN hullo little amy – don't you look pretty in that apron – no sugar for you – you're sweet enough ey ey

AMY hello mr casey

UNCLE RYAN lot of people here today need to get more chairs from out back – come help me

AMY i have to pour the tea

UNCLE RYAN suit yerself – i'll take a biscuit meantime

AMY up at the front a man from the council – hair slicked and shining suit – jacket and trousers don't quite match – face like a red balloon tied tight with long green tie

COUNCILLOR yes i can assure you – absolutely assure you – that we are doing – everything we can – everything – to to listen to your concerns – whilst working – working closely – tirelessly – with local authorities and the government to to –

AMY mutterings and murmurings

MRS M the government

BOBBY'S MUM the government

UNCLE RYAN what do they know

MR PATEL never work always shirk

FISHBAR JIM the fields are shut

BOBBY'S DAD no fields no farm no work no money

MS H i can't run a riding school with nowhere to ride

AMY'S MUM farm shop closing – i've to go to swindon now for a few eggs

FISHBAR JIM i'm losing customers

MR PATEL i'm losing customers

MS H i'm losing customers

AMY even the goats

GOATS KELLY AND TIFF we're so bored

GOAT STACE bored

COUNCILLOR we will listen to all your concerns but right now – right now it's imperative we – as i say we are in touch with the government

BOBBY'S DAD no fields no farm no work no money

MRS M spineless snivelling toads

BOBBY'S MUM when will ya open the fields

MS H when will you open the fields

BOBBY'S DAD no fields no farm no work no money

COUNCILLOR once we have done a thorough – thorough assessment of the situation we will –

SLAYER SLATER what about my dad

BOBBY silence – slayer slater stood up straight out of folding plastic – everyone looks at him he looks at his feet and speaks again

SLAYER SLATER what about my dad – all your shouting but what about – our whole farm our whole – everything – burned – fucking –

BOBBY farmer rog puts a hand on his arm

FARMER ROG it's alright lad – sit down

BOBBY slayer sniffs and sways then slides and strides across parquet floor and through door – the goats and tuck follow

AMY bobby's mum tells us to go wash up – we sneak out back behind bins and head past the church – kels and slayer tonguing on a tombstone

GOAT KELLY aw kenny

SLAYER SLATER awwww kels

GOAT KELLY kenny you still crying

SLAYER SLATER just keep going

GOAT KELLY but

SLAYER SLATER keep going

GOAT KELLY my arm's getting tired

SLAYER SLATER change hands – aww kel

GOAT KELLY aw kenny (*to* **BOBBY** *and* **AMY**) what you looking at

AMY dart away –

BOBBY what were they doing

AMY nothing

BOBBY work work never shirk – morning mr patel

MR PATEL bobby i need to speak to you

BOBBY you are speaking to me mr patel

MR PATEL bobby – business has been bad

BOBBY i know mr patel

MR PATEL people can't pay for their prescriptions and purchases
are down

BOBBY yes mr patel – purchases are down by thirty eight point
seven per cent

MR PATEL i need to make savings bobby

BOBBY but what savings mr patel – you've already changed lots

MR PATEL i know bobby – i am sad very sad because i am going
to have to let you go

BOBBY go where

MR PATEL i cannot pay you bobby

BOBBY oh

MR PATEL i am very sorry

BOBBY i can work harder

MR PATEL that will not help

BOBBY oh

MR PATEL i can pay you till the end of the week

BOBBY yes mr patel – ok mr patel – work work never shirk
mr patel

MR PATEL work work never shirk bobby

BOBBY i lost my job daddy

BOBBY'S DAD join the fuckin' club – here have a drink

BOBBY but i don't drink daddy

BOBBY'S DADDY the world is fucked bobby – fucked – when a man can't pay the bills in his own home – look after his own land – right rog

BOBBY farmer rog hello farmer rog

FARMER ROG *(downs his drink)* – another one ed

BOBBY can i have a job fishbar jim

FISHBAR JIM no jobs 'ere – only frozen chips and packet pies – can't get nothing fresh – no one's got a penny

BOBBY can i have a job ms huntington-smythe

MS H gracious me – a job – i've let two stable hands go this year already – no bloody horses left – until they let us back in the fields i'm stuck in that stable with nothing but salt licks and saddle soap for company

BOBBY you could pay me less

MS H know anything about horses

BOBBY i know about cows

AMY a year passes – citizens stranded in streets – closing down sales – fishbar jim is packing up and movin' to swindon – farm shop only has tins and stamps – the town feels – one day in co-op – shop bell ding ding

BOBBY amy amy the tape is coming off

AMY what

BOBBY the tape – they're taking it down

AMY what really

BOBBY we can go in the fields – we can go to the folly – we can see farmer rog we can help with the farm – we can go help him make things like they were – come on

AMY bobby i'm at work

BOBBY but the tape is off the tape is off

AMY i know but i can't just

BOBBY amy – the – tape – is – off

AMY ok ok

BOBBY amy throws off her tabard – turns the sign

AMY and we're running

BOBBY we're running – off up the farm to see farmer rog

AMY up to the fields

BOBBY farmer rog farmer rog

AMY farmer rog

BOBBY farmer rog

AMY up to the barn

BOBBY farmer rog

AMY up to the house

BOBBY farmer rog – slayer – slayer slater and tuck – faces hard and wet

SLAYER SLATER what you want

TUCK yeh what you want wobot

AMY we were looking for your dad

BOBBY they've taken the tape off

SLAYER SLATER yeh no shit

TUCK no shit

AMY we want to see farmer rog

BOBBY we want to see farmer rog

SLAYER SLATER yeh well you can't see 'im so fuck off

TUCK yeh fuck off and leave thlayer awone

AMY can we come back later

BOBBY can we come back later

SLAYER SLATER yeh you can come back later but it won't make a fuckin' difference

TUCK fuckin' differenth

BOBBY but the tape's off –

SLAYER SLATER i fuckin' know the tape's off

BOBBY when's he back – we can help get more cows and –

SLAYER SLATER listen don't you get it – he's not coming back

BOBBY where's he gone

SLAYER SLATER he's gone up the folly – you can find him there – go on – find him there

BOBBY over the fields – folly in the distance

AMY folly getting closer

BOBBY through the barbed fences

AMY bobby's in front

BOBBY folly getting nearer

AMY nearer

BOBBY nearer

AMY i can see some rubbish

BOBBY a pile of rubbish

AMY swinging from the tower

BOBBY a pile of rubbish or some old bags

AMY some old bags or some old clothes – there's a welly

BOBBY two wellies

AMY and a hat

BOBBY like farmer rog's hat

AMY and legs

BOBBY like farmer rog's legs

AMY dark black wellies dark green coat dark grey cap – dangling dangling –

BOBBY farmer rog farmer rog

AMY bobby no

BOBBY farmer rog farmer rog

AMY bobby no don't

BOBBY dark black wellies dark green coat and dark grey cap – purple skin and yellow smile and bright white lips swinging in the breeze

AMY farmer rog

BOBBY neck stretched – rope taut tight

AMY bending beam creaking and shrieking as body bumps brick and toes tip to ground – paper catches – bobby the paper

BOBBY what

AMY catch the paper – it flits and twists

BOBBY and i run and catch

AMY it flew out from his coat – from farmer rog's coat

BOBBY *(reading)* kenny

FARMER ROG kenny lad – forty-five years i cared for this land – caring for the land and the animals on that land is what give me most joy – my father always said that farmin' is an art – it's what holds this fast and changing world together – i know it aint got the glamour or what have you but i always hoped i brought you up to know that there's nowt better than getting the earth on your hands and breathing the rain – remember that son – fifteen generations our family 'ave been on this land – i felt my heart burn on that bonfire along with all them cattle we worked so hard to rear – i've tried i have but it won't stop burning – the world's changing so fast and it don't want the likes of me in it no more – this land is yours now – maybe you can bring it the glory it once had – i'm sorry son – it's better this way – take care of ya mother

AMY oh bobby

BOBBY whirring siren and blue flashing lights

AMY bobby bobby come away now come away

AMY sharp sun splices stone and starches – body wrapped in polished pine and brass edging – lowered down beneath the earth

BOBBY slayer stands silent with his mum margery – tuck tucked up in tailored suit and shoes – the goats wobble in black heels across the mud – everyone is here

AMY bobby's mum helps with the flowers – she winces when she waters

BOBBY where's daddy mummy

BOBBY'S MUM your father and me we're taking some time apart darling – he'll be along later i'm sure

BOBBY amy's mum stands snotting into white lilies – uncle ryan's arm wrapped round her – we ring round the hollow hole – hard handfuls of earth pour and plummet on to pine and printed plaque – we say a prayer then walk away – hello daddy

BOBBY'S DAD alright bobby – so that's him in there is it –

BOBBY yes daddy

BOBBY'S DAD i don't blame him bobby – your mum here

BOBBY she's gone to set up sandwiches

BOBBY'S DAD course she fuckin' has

AMY town hall – i hand round cucumber sandwiches and iceland party platters – the goats bleat in a corner

The GOAT*s laugh.*

GOAT KELLY and what with farmer rog's debts he jumped at the chance –

GOAT TIFF no way

GOAT STACE no way

GOAT KELLY way – he's gonna take me on holiday with the money from the sale – marbella – gonna be lush

AMY what – sale

GOAT KELLY uh this is a private conversation

AMY sale what sale

GOAT KELLY duh the farm – a company's building new houses on kenny's land – proper modern they are – well lush – like i said to kenny – what's the point of keeping that shit hole going – it'd take decades to build up that herd again

AMY slayer's selling the farm

GOAT KELLY yeh duh

GOAT TIFF duh

GOAT STACE duh

AMY the platter plummets and crustless cucumber crashes on to carpet – my face gets hot and wet and and – i run – i hear bobby shout in the distance but i run – out the hall away from the handkerchiefs and huddled hushes – i run past the fish shop the shutting down fish shop – i run past the co-op the boarded up co-op – i run past the pharmacy the closing down pharmacy – and i run – past tombstones and graves and rotting roses and contaminated carnations – up against cold stone gothic stone and through doors giant doors – i fall on to coldness and hardness – wooden benches all around and i cry into crosses on cushions – into doves and daisies – into altars and angels – all woven and scratching – the man selling postcards doesn't know what to do – he goes out for a cigarette the door shuts and it's quiet – my breath echoes on stone and columns – it swoops through organ pipes and bounces off pulpits and i turn around and through my tears there's this light through the enormous old etched and leaded window – horrible faces horrible clawing toothed and screaming red and black – faces on stomachs and stomachs on faces and hooves and horns and blood and burning blood – i want to scream like them in the heat and the horror –

and then the light moves and i see different faces – and gold and blues and light and fields and peace and happiness – and the light glows in my face and it bleaches me – it bleaches the feelings the stains and the spills – kitchen sink bleach and drain cleaner clean – and that's where i want to be – i want to be there with that nice man on the throne and his nice friends all smiling with the sheep and the happiness and the blue and the gold – it looks so nice in the blue and the gold –

BOBBY amy amy are you ok

AMY they're selling the farm bobby

BOBBY what

AMY they're selling the farm for new houses

BOBBY no – they can't –

AMY why is everything so unfair bobby – why can everyone else do whatever they want – whenever they want – except us

BOBBY back through town hall door amy and me push past making mourners move

AMY hello hello – um –

BOBBY mutterings and murmurings

AMY sorry – but –

TUCK look da twoll and da wickle wobot

AMY'S MUM amy get down now

UNCLE RYAN what you doin' pretty amy

SLAYER SLATER get down you retard

GOAT KELLY kenny what they doing up there

GOAT TIFF like oh my god

GOAT STACE my tamagotchi's hungry – huh

AMY i'm sorry – but they're selling the farm – and and they're going to build houses on it – all those lovely fields and and – um – oh – what am i doing– um – sorry i

She looks to **BOBBY**.

BOBBY it's not fair

AMY yes it's not fair

BOBBY they killed the cows – killed abigail – and they took our fields and farmer rog – and now

AMY exactly – if they get rid of the farm and all those fields and the folly then it won't be our town at all any more – and i just – i think it's sad and and – anyway that's what i wanted to say – sorry

BOBBY tilted faces stare – so many faces – suddenly

BOBBY'S DAD well fuckin' said – well fuckin' –

FISHBAR JIM bang on – good on yer – bang on

BOBBY'S DAD here here rog wouldn't want the farm to go

MRS M i grew up playing in that folly – caw caw

BOBBY'S MUM i love that folly

MS H jolly good show what what

AMY'S MUM and i did too – didn't i ryan

UNCLE RYAN we've all had good times in that there folly

BOBBY'S DAD what do you have to say for yerself kenneth – your father must be turning in his grave

BOBBY room goes silent – slayer shuffles

SLAYER SLATER yeh well if he cared that much about anything then he shouldn't have topped himself should he

BOBBY door slam sandwiches shake

AMY silence

FISHBAR JIM caused quite a stir 'aven't ya

AMY i'm sorry i didn't mean –

BOBBY we didn't mean –

BOBBY'S DAD good on both of ya

FISHBAR JIM hear hear

BOBBY'S DAD good on both of ya

FISHBAR JIM hear hear bang on

AMY sleepy town wide awake

BOBBY placards in the market square – please sign the petition – handing out flyers – letters to the council – my daddy makes speeches in the pub

BOBBY'S DAD fuck 'em's wot i say – we're gonna show them they can't just swan in and take what's ours – my son here – stand up son – this young lad knew it before any of us – didn't you – he knew it first – he has more bollocks than the rest of you put together don't you son

BOBBY amy knew it first daddy and then i –

BOBBY'S DAD three cheers for my lad's bollocks – hip hip – *(hiccups and staggers)* fuck me

BOBBY local secondary school – up the lane – iron gates shield of blue and gold – nine hundred navy jumpers holding signs and making banners – boys' voices high then low then low then squeak

KID 2 save our farm dumbarses

KID 1 yeh save it weirdos – hi stacey – you like our signs

KID 2 *(mimicking)* hi stacey like our signs

GOAT STACE umm – hi

AMY two pairs of black leather kickers – laces tucked in

GOAT KELLY stace what you doin'

GOAT TIFF yeh what you doin'

GOAT STACE nothing

KID 1 stace i was thinking yeh – if you ever like – want me to look after your tamagotchi – tammy – like – give you a break – or or we could look after it together

GOAT STACE tammy would like that

GOAT TIFF stacey

GOAT KELLY stacey – what you doing talking to those losers

GOAT TIFF yeh losers

GOAT STACE nothing

GOAT KELLY who's side are you on

GOAT TIFF yeh – who's side

GOAT STACE i just – nothing

AMY the local newspaper comes to talk to us – they take photos of our banners – they want to interview me and bobby – i'm too scared

BOBBY so amy's mummy speaks to them instead

AMY'S MUM oh i'm just so upset aren't i ryan just so upset about what they're doing – and as soon as i heard about the sale – as soon as i heard i said we should do something – and things have been tough but – well look – we're engaged – he proposed last night – so every cloud – could you take one on my left side you can get the ring in then –

BOBBY you ok amy

AMY i need more flyers

BOBBY we get so many signatures the councillor comes back to town

AMY we squeeze into the town hall – no room for folding plastic chairs or clinking crockery – balloon face inflated bigger than before –

COUNCILLOR yes yes i can assure you – that we will – will listen to your concerns – whilst working closely – with the developers to to

AMY mutterings and murmerings

MRS M the developers pah

BOBBY'S DAD the developers fuck 'em

COUNCILLOR – the redevelopment of the farm land is the best thing that can be done in in consideration of the recent change in in economic circumstances within the town – and all new building will be in keeping with the area's – local aesthetic – there will also be a tesco and and

AMY'S MUM a tesco – i love tesco don't i ryan

COUNCILLOR other amenities built within the complex and i am sure –

MR PATEL those buildings are listed – the folly must be six hundred years old at least

COUNCILLOR the council agreed that in its current condition it is a public health hazard and the cost –

BOBBY'S DAD they paid you off

COUNCILLOR i can assure you that –

BOBBY'S MUM how can any one afford to live in them new houses – who has a swimming pool in their garden

FISHBAR JIM you getting a swimming pool councillor

AMY'S MUM ryan i always wanted a swimming pool

COUNCILLOR i am sorry but the demolition of the farm and surrounding buildings will be beginning tomorrow as scheduled – that is all

AMY the councillor steps off the stage – slayer smiles and shakes his hand

BOBBY bodies left heaving and hollering but eventually there's nothing to say – amy – amy are you ok

AMY why is everything taken away from me bobby why is everything always taken away –

BOBBY i'm not being taken away amy

AMY i can't stop crying – why can't i stop crying

BOBBY is that ok amy – your face is very symmetrical when you cry

AMY what

BOBBY it's symmetrical

AMY my nose is big

BOBBY but it's the same on both sides – i like it

AMY no you don't

BOBBY scientists say symmetry is the most beautiful thing in nature

AMY you think i'm beautiful

BOBBY you must be – you're symmetrical

AMY i think you're beautiful too

BOBBY i'm not symmetrical

AMY it doesn't matter

BOBBY yes it does

AMY come on let's go

BOBBY where

AMY out back by the fields is the old folly – bright stone barbed wire and buttercups – inside a rickety ladder reaching raw to a platform so high up – at top the sunset shoots and splices through a single window – the purple and orange of fields and skies

BOBBY amy abigail's dead

AMY yes

BOBBY and farmer rog

AMY yes

BOBBY and now the farm is going

AMY yes

BOBBY i don't understand

AMY sometimes bad things happen – and sometimes things have to change

BOBBY why

AMY i don't know

BOBBY the sun sets behind the hill – shadows spread stars come out and wink and blink at the thin blue moon – red sky at night

AMY sleep tight

BOBBY we wake to sharp sun eating eyelids and a roaring rumbling beeping sound

AMY bobby what's going on

BOBBY look

AMY we look out the window and down below yellow plastic and rusted metal and giant claw sneak shaking and screaming in front of our folly

BOBBY big plastic man in little plastic hat peering through plastic panes – metal moving forward churning ground and grass

AMY oh my god

BOBBY they're about to knock it down

AMY and us with it – stop stop

BOBBY stop stop

AMY stop stop

BOBBY stop stop

BUILDER what the shit

BOBBY giant claw screeches to stop and hangs in the air

BUILDER you fuckin' mental – i could've killed you – shittin' 'ell

BOBBY the builder shakes his head – he picks up a big black brick and spits something into it – robot voices talk back

BUILDER will do – over and out

BOBBY he turns a key and engine stops

BUILDER cheers kids – i'm paid by the hour

BOBBY he's leaving – why's he leaving

AMY he can't knock it down if we're in here

BOBBY so he's waiting for us to leave

AMY i think so – the sun moves higher in the sky and the wind warms – engine in the distance – a sleek black car comes over the hill

BOBBY who's that

AMY angry eyebrows slide out from car seats fists gripped teeth tight

BOBBY oh no

SLAYER SLATER what the fuck you think you're doing – get out of there now before i pound you into a picasso – prick

COUNCILLOR yes thank you mr slater perhaps i should deal with this – it is my duty to inform you that you are trespassing on private property –

SLAYER SLATER yeh you pussy – private property –

COUNCILLOR and this this – protest – is entirely illegal – as i said last night the council's decision is final

SLAYER SLATER fucking final you shitting spaztic

COUNCILLOR mr slater please – as such i have had no choice but to call the police

AMY he's going to have us arrested – bobby what do we do

BOBBY we can't leave – they'll take the folly

AMY you're right – we have to try to save it

BOBBY so we're staying

AMY we're staying

BOBBY we wait

AMY we wait

BOBBY siren in the distance blue flashing lights

AMY the police are coming

BOBBY the police are coming

AMY oh bobby i'm scared

BOBBY so am i amy – what's that over the hill

AMY people running

BOBBY it's the town – the whole town –

AMY ms huntington-smythe pulls out in front – nostrils flaring she looks ready to spit blood – bumping bumping – her four hooves spit mud

MS H ya ya – stop stop

AMY hooves pounding pounding then skid to a stop

MS H woah lady woah – you leave those young things alone you – you want to destroy this land you'll have to get through me

AMY others catching up

BOBBY daddy

BOBBY'S DAD aye and me – you alright up there bobby

BOBBY yes daddy

AMY mrs m

MRS M you pathetic pieces of pernicious putridness – you flaccid fucking flotsams – i'll make you masticate on melancholy if you fry a feather on these young birds' heads – caw caw – opal fruit –

AMY oh yes please mrs m

BOBBY mummy

BOBBY'S MUM bobby darling – are you alright up there

BOBBY yes mummy

BOBBY'S MUM i love you darling – you're being very brave

BOBBY love you too mummy

AMY the goats arrive bleating louder than before

GOAT KELLY like oh my god what is the troll doing

GOAT TIFF like what is she doing

BOBBY but stacey

AMY stacey

GOAT STACE hi amy hi bobby i think what you're doing is really great

    GOATS KELLY *and* **TIFF** *look shocked.*

AMY thanks stacey – heads shake and wax hats gleam beneath us as bodies and bodies wrap round the folly in front of the pulling up police cars – they start to chant and we join in

THE TOWN save our folly – save our folly

BOBBY slayer slater and bulging balloon face back up to boys in blue – words whipped by the wind and skimmed past our ears too quick for us to hear

THE TOWN save our folly save our folly

AMY a policeman steps forward and comes towards the crowd – oh no – bobby what's going to happen

BOBBY i don't know

AMY he goes up to bobby's daddy

POLICEMAN dave

BOBBY'S DAD ian – long time

POLICEMAN so they trying to knock this down are they

BOBBY'S DAD aye

POLICEMAN had me first kiss up there – you set on stopping 'em

BOBBY'S DAD 'fraid so mate

POLICEMAN alright

AMY policeman turns to balloon face and slayer

POLICEMAN sorry sir – peaceful protest – nothing we can do

AMY balloon face inflates until his feet almost leave the ground

BOBBY amy – they can't make us leave

AMY the town start chanting again – more and more people join – from somewhere cake and tea appears – all day – the town chanting like it's a party – slayer and balloon face drive away

BOBBY we keep chanting

AMY the sun sets

BOBBY we keep chanting

AMY it gets dark

BOBBY the chants get quieter

AMY people go home for their tea

BOBBY then there's just me and amy

AMY then there's just me and bobby – up in our folly

BOBBY we've only eaten opal fruits and a slice of cake since yesterday

AMY it's getting cold

BOBBY really cold

AMY do you think they're coming back

BOBBY who

AMY the town

BOBBY i don't know

AMY i'm sure they are

BOBBY i'm sure they are

AMY they are – out back by the fields is the place where the old folly used to be – grey and white houses polka dot the distance with range rovers and mercedes sat fat on gravelled drives

BOBBY the blue and the green of mediterranean pots and mown grass

AMY the sun shoots and splices through shimmering conservatories and there are signs saying – holiday lets enquire within

BOBBY a new boots pharmacy opened up in the market square

AMY and mummies with pearl earrings and daddies in suits eat at the italian restaurant

BOBBY amy and me are older now

AMY we live in mrs m's house – ivy crawling through crack and cove – she left it to us when she died – the whole house filled with sweet wrappers

BOBBY amy works in the new art gallery – i stack shelves in tesco

AMY i walk down the market place – empty during the week – at the weekend filled with faces i've never seen – they say they come for the views i say they've all been built on now

BOBBY nothing's the same here any more

AMY nothing's the same

BOBBY but still every evening

AMY every evening

BOBBY when the sky turns gold and the land turns blue

AMY bobby and i take a walk to where the old folly used to be

BOBBY it's a carpark now

AMY we go to a corner – just behind the ticket machine

BOBBY where there's a small stone sign in a drystone wall

AMY and we look at the beautiful letters

BOBBY in loving memory

AMY in loving memory of farmer rog

BOBBY in loving memory of farmer rog – and abigail

VISIT THE
SAMUEL FRENCH
BOOKSHOP
AT THE
ROYAL COURT THEATRE

Browse plays and theatre books, get expert advice and enjoy a coffee

Samuel French Bookshop
Royal Court Theatre
Sloane Square
London
SW1W 8AS
020 7565 5024

Shop from thousands of titles on our website

 samuelfrench.co.uk

 samuelfrenchltd

 samuel french uk

9 780573 116735